布達拉宮

赵朴初题

THE POTALA PALACE
OF LHASA

南卉编

Compiled by Nan Hui

中国世界语出版社

Published by China Esperanto Press, Beijing

First edition: August 1995

ISBN 7-5052 − 0243 − X
Published by China Esperanto Press, Beijing
Distributed by China International Book Trading Corporation
35 W. Chegongzhuang Xilu, Beijing China
P. O. Box 399, Post code: 100044
Printed in the People's Republic of China

目　录

CONTENTS

"世界屋脊"上的圣殿——布达拉宫

萧　辰

每当旅游者和朝圣者进入拉萨河谷的德庆宗地界时，便可远远望见布达拉宫的金顶在蓝天下闪烁着耀眼的光辉。此时，人们兴奋、欢呼、雀跃，而信徒们则更为虔诚，甚至增添了几分敬畏，因为这里距离他们前去朝觐的圣地布达拉宫已不到30公里的路程了。

布达拉宫所在的西藏自治区首府拉萨市座落在雅鲁藏布江支流拉萨河北岸，海拔3700米，是一座具有1300多年历史的古城。因为它的日照时间一年长达3000多小时，所以又有"日光城"之称。布达拉宫修筑在市内的红山上，城堡式的殿宇依山就势，层层叠叠，以其坚固的城垣，把红山的上半部包裹得严严实实。从墙壁的外表看，布达拉宫分为红色和白色两部分。红色部分称为"红宫"，其建筑特点是，既有女儿墙围护的藏式平顶，又有飞檐凌空的汉式金顶。白色部分称为"白宫"，它环抱红宫而建，砌在山岩之上的墙体陡峭雄浑，仿佛把红宫高高托起。由红山脚下到白宫墙根，高约100米，人们沿着曲折的磴道拾级而上，通过坐西面东的宫门，进入宫城，一座座华丽而神秘的殿堂便展现在眼前，这些殿堂错落有致，由廊道和扶梯里外相连，上下相通，形成一个庞大的整体。其中主楼13层，高117.9米，东西长360余米，南北宽270米，面积约13万平方米，巍峨雄峙，令人赞叹不已。

据史书记载，布达拉宫始建于公元7世纪中叶。那时候，西藏高原出现了一位有胆有识有作为的赞普松赞干布（公元617？～650年）。他统一了西藏境内各部落，建立了吐蕃王朝（公元7～9世纪西藏地区政权）。为了睦邻友好，他先娶尼泊尔的尺尊公主为妻，后又于公元641年迎娶唐朝宗室女文成公主（？～680年），并在红山上"别建宫室，以居公主"。当时修筑的宫殿规模相当宏大，在红山周围用巨石砌了三道城墙，在城墙内构筑宫室999间，加上松赞干布先前在这里修行的一间洞式建筑，共计1000间。这些宫室内部饰以各色珍宝，琳琅满目，外部廊檐悬挂一行行铃铎，山风吹过，叮当作响。据说在主楼宫殿与王妃宫室之间还架设了用银或铜铸成的桥梁，以便行走平直快捷。可惜这些精美建筑的大部分后来毁于兵燹和雷击。斗转星移，待历史发展到公元13世纪，西藏地方已统一于元朝的版图，红山也已成为藏传佛教的主要活动场所。公元17世纪中叶，五世达赖喇嘛罗桑嘉措（1617～1682年）建立噶丹颇章政权以后，考虑到红山所处位置的重要，决定筹划将设在哲蚌寺的政权机构逐步移往红山，并特派他的助手第司·索朗热登于公元 1645 年开始重建布达拉宫。重建时规划，以松赞干布时期的修法洞和本尊观音佛堂为中心，向东西两侧展开，兴建白宫，历时八年竣工。公元 1653 年，五世达赖喇嘛从北京觐见清朝顺治皇帝（1643～1661 年在位）归来，目睹布达拉宫重新崛起于红山之巅，心潮澎湃，深感佛的崇高伟大，即将自己的宫室和政权机构由哲蚌寺移入布达拉宫。三十八年后的公元 1690 年，布达拉宫再次大兴土木，历时三年，在白宫的上部中心区兴建了红宫的主体建筑。同时建造灵塔，用以安放已在八年前圆寂的五世达赖喇嘛的尸骸。此后，历代达赖喇嘛对布达拉宫都有过增修和改建，从而形成今天的规模。

现今游览或朝觐布达拉宫的最佳路线，是由宫前磴道登临，进东大门，再穿行 4 米厚的宫墙隧道，首先到达德阳厦。德阳厦是一个面积约 1600 平方米的广场，每逢节日或庆典活动在这里演出藏戏和歌舞。由德阳厦西端沿梯而上，是通往各个殿堂的廊道。这个廊道其实是个古老的画廊。四壁绘有壁画，其中东墙面画的是唐朝都城长安图、唐皇五难吐蕃婚使图，北墙面画的是唐文成公主进藏图。顺廊道而行，即进入东大殿。这座大殿建于公元 1645 年，是白宫最大的殿堂，四十八根大柱支撑着它那巨大的殿顶。由于光线不很充足，使得大殿更显高崇而深幽，平添几分神秘。公元 1653 年，五世达赖喇嘛受到顺治皇帝的册封，领受了金册金印。从此以后，历代达赖喇嘛必须得到中央政府的册封，并由中央政府派驻西藏的大臣在东大殿为其主持坐床、亲政等仪式。东大殿也是达赖喇嘛举行重大宗教活动和政治活动的地方。白宫的最高处为达赖喇嘛的寝宫，俗称日光殿，有东西两组，分别称为东日光殿、西日光殿。殿内设有经堂、习经堂、会客厅和

卧室，存放着达赖喇嘛用过的金银器皿、珠宝珍玩，十分豪华。达赖喇嘛亲政后，在西日光殿的经堂内"早朝"，接见高级僧官；俗官未经召唤不得入内，只能在殿外廊下静候。日光殿外有宽敞的平台，达赖及其随官，余暇时，常登上平台，或远眺巍巍群山，或俯看拉萨城里人来车往和袅袅炊烟。

离开白宫，进入红宫，红宫的主体建筑是达赖喇嘛的灵塔殿和佛堂。灵塔殿共有八座，顶部覆盖着鎏金的铜瓦，装饰着鎏金的铜顶、宝瓶、神鲸，以及法轮、经幢等。八座灵塔殿中，五世达赖喇嘛的是第一座，也是最大的一座；十三世达赖喇嘛（1876～1933 年）的是最后一座，也是最新的一座。一般来说，瞻仰过这两座灵塔殿，基本上能够饱眼福，了心愿。五世达赖喇嘛灵塔殿的享堂是红宫最大的殿堂，这里保存着一对清康熙皇帝（1661～1722 年在位）赐予的大幅锦绣帐幔。据说为了制作这对帐幔，专门建立了一间作坊，费时一年才完工。每当达赖喇嘛举行坐床、亲政大典时，这对帐幔就悬挂在大殿的显要位置，一方面炫耀此物是皇帝所赐，另一方面为庆典增添几分庄重气氛。五世达赖喇嘛的灵塔殿位于大殿以西，灵塔就在殿内，塔高 14.85 米，为梯形的塔座、宝瓶形的塔体、尖形的塔顶。整座灵塔裹以金箔，用珠玉宝石镶嵌成各种图案。据有关书籍记载，建造这座灵塔共用去黄金 3721 公斤，白银 32557 公斤，珍珠、翡翠、玛瑙和其他宝石数以万计。塔内除五世达赖喇嘛的遗骸外，还有 19180 公斤青稞和小麦，难以数计的酥油、茶叶、檀香木、宝石、绸缎和经书。红宫最西面是十三世达赖喇嘛的灵塔殿，修建于 1934 年至 1936 年间。殿堂分三层，最上层绘满壁画，内容为十三世达赖喇嘛的生平事迹。十三世达赖喇嘛的灵塔高约 14 米，同样是全身裹以金箔，缀以宝石。塔体正面有

一道"眼光门"，塔内用一扇窗格分成里外间。外间设佛龛，供奉十一面千手千眼观音菩萨像。里间有佛床，床顶有天棚，床后有帐幔，床上有被褥、枕头和一口木箱，箱内是身着法衣的十三世达赖喇嘛的遗骸；床前桌上摆着他生前用过的各种法器、经书、墨瓶和竹笔等。在灵塔旁边，人们还能看到一座精巧的"曼陀罗"，即坛场，是用20多万颗珍珠、珊瑚珠串编而成的。坛场的底盘是"轮王七室"，中心是方塔形四层梯，顶端置一幢金质宫阁，阁内供奉一尊31公斤重的银铸十三世达赖喇嘛像，外部四周饰挂着用珍珠、珊瑚珠串缀而成的璎珞。

由西大殿登上二层，又是一条古老的画廊。一组组壁画生动真实地再现了当年修建红宫的情景，有很高的研究价值。再由此上行，便是松赞干布的修法洞。它是布达拉宫最为古老的建筑，已有1300多年历史，至今仍保存着松赞干布、文成公主、尺尊公主和他们的近臣的塑像。这些塑像造型丰满、线条柔畅，相传是吐蕃时期的作品。修法洞楼上是圣观音殿，也是布达拉宫的早期建筑，主供自在观音菩萨雕像，相传为松赞干布的本尊佛。五世达赖喇嘛曾在这里坐禅修法，顺治皇帝赐给他的八尊檀香木佛像也供奉在这里。

红宫的最高殿堂是"殊胜三界"，也叫三界兴盛殿，建于公元1679年，位置正好是布达拉宫的中心。殿内主供七世达赖喇嘛（1708～1757年）请来的康熙皇帝的长生牌位。牌位后面，悬挂着由八世达赖喇嘛（1758～1804年）请来的乾隆皇帝（1735～1795年在位）佛妆画像唐卡。每逢藏历新年和皇帝生日，历世达赖喇嘛都到此向皇帝的牌位和画像朝拜，真可谓"普天之下，莫非王土。率土之滨，莫非王臣"，皇帝在布达拉宫的位置同样是至高无上的。

屹立于红山之巅的布达拉宫是藏传佛教僧徒心目中的圣地，同时也是中国罕见的具有鲜明藏族特色的大型古典建筑群遗存，是世界文化的瑰宝。

这组建筑群是宫殿与寺庙相结合的典范，是为适应西藏历史上政教合一制度的需要而修建的。从外表看，梯形建筑轮廓的房屋互相依附，造成威严磅礴的气势，从而达到对神的尊崇和对人的威慑的目的，这就是布达拉宫的建筑奥秘。在内部结构上，既有不同等级人员的生活起居设施，又有颁施政令的各种政权机构，还有举行大型宗教活动和供众多喇嘛进行严格修习的场所，整体布局规整有序。在设计和建造方法上，充分考虑到了高原寒冷和多发地震的地理环境因素，因此外围裹以厚墙。数米厚的墙基向下砌在天然的岩石上，向上逐渐收缩，稳定性极强。墙的内层全部采用木结构建筑，与墙体之间留出空隙，起着保温作用。由于在修建的过程中，除有大量藏族能工巧匠参加外，还吸收了汉族、蒙古族和尼泊尔的工匠。这些能工巧匠在宫殿的设计、外型的装饰、壁画的绘制、图案的表现等方面，都贡献了自己的力量和才华，使得布达拉宫这座藏式建筑同时具有某些汉族、蒙古族和尼泊尔国的建筑风格。

布达拉宫陈设华丽，珍藏着大量文物、珠宝和贵重物品。整个宫殿有大小金雕、玉雕、铜雕、木雕、石雕佛像上万尊，还有"唐卡"佛像、木版画佛像不计其数，其中许多堪称艺术杰作。那处处可见的壁画和梁柱上的彩绘究竟有多少幅，没有精确的统计，仅红宫二楼回廊就有壁画698幅。这些绘画许多至今依然色泽鲜艳，向人们讲述着佛的伟大、神的崇高、达赖喇嘛的功德、藏汉两族人民和睦相处友好交往等许许多多的故事。宫内的经卷堆积如山，其中有最早从印度流传到西藏的用针在叶片上刺写的经文"贝叶经"，有用金粉写成的佛经《甘珠尔》和用金、银、松耳石、珊瑚、海螺等研磨成汁水写成的佛经注疏和《丹珠尔》，共 100 余部。至于自元（1271～1368 年）以来中央政府敕封给西藏地方官员的印鉴、诏诰、玉册以及那些具有历史价值和艺术价值的法器、经幡、藏毯、帐幔等器物，更是数不胜数。

中国政府和中国人民对于布达拉宫这颗"世界屋脊"的明珠十分珍惜和爱护，列为全国重点文物保护单位，成立专门机构加以保护，每年拨专款进行维修。但是，布达拉宫毕竟经历了漫长岁月的风侵雨蚀、虫蛀鼠咬、烟熏火燎，出现了种种险情。1988 年，中国政府决定维修布达拉宫，成立了专家技术小组，经过三个多月的实地勘测，制定出总体维修方案，投入巨资维修七十七个项目，总面积达到 2.8 万平方米。1989 年 10 月维修工程开工，一支以藏族工匠为主的施工队，严格遵循"尊重科学，尊重传统，尊重民族风格，尊重宗教需要"的原则，历时近五年，圆满完成了维修方案所规定的项目。原先出现裂隙的墙体弥合加固了，糟朽的梁椽抽旧换新了，被熏黑的壁画经过清洗又露出了鲜艳的颜色，危害最大的火险隐患得到排除，而宫内的文物宝器却没有一件损坏或丢失，全部复位如初。最令人称绝的是维修加固五世达赖喇嘛的灵塔殿时，藏汉工匠和技师共出奇招，在不拆除梁架和金顶的情况下，进行加固排险，保留了原物、原状、原貌。经过精心维修之后，这座布达拉宫最高的灵塔殿金顶牢牢地屹立于高原雪域，在蓝天丽日之下，闪烁着更加耀眼的光辉。

The Potala Palace of Lhasa
—a Sanctuary on the 'Roof of the World'

by Xiao Chen

Lhasa, capital of Tibet Autonomous Region, is under sunshine for 3,000 hours a year, so it is also called "City of Sunshine". It has preserved many historical relics and ancient buildings through its history of 1,300 years. The most famous is the Potala Palace.

The 13-story Potala Palace in the heart of old Lhasa city rises up the south wall of the Red Mountain 3,700 meters above sea level, making it the highest Buddhist sanctuary in the world. Its lofty roofs with gilded copper tiles present a magnificent sight as far as 30 kilometers away in the Lhasa River Valley, giving much comfort to travelers and pilgrims making their way to the holy place.

The Potala Palace is composed of two parts: the White Palace and the Red Palace. Stone stairs lead to the eastern gate and a platform 100 meters up the hill. The palace wall is up to five meters thick. Corridors and stairways connect the various halls and chambers up and down.

On a graded foundation, the Hall of Avalokitesvara, main building of the palace, rises 117.9 meters against the southern slope of the hill. It is 360 meters long from east to west and 270 meters wide from south to north, and covers a floor space of 130,000 square meters.

In the seventh century Songtsan Gambo (617-650) unified Tibet and founded the Tubo regime. He built the Potala Palace for his bride, Princess Wencheng of the Tang Dynasty in central China. The construction included three thick walls of huge stone blocks and 999 rooms. The king had studied Buddhist scriptures on the Red Mountain in a cave-dwelling. So the total number of rooms with the cave-dwelling came to 1,000. The halls and chambers were all decorated with precious ornaments. Bells hung from their eaves. A bridge of silver and copper spanned the space between the main building and the living quarters of the king's two wives. But little is left of the original palace, it having been twice destroyed by lightning and war.

The Potala Palace we see today was reconstructed in 1645 by Lozang Gyatso, the fifth Dalai Lama (1617-1682) who founded the Ganden Phodrang regime in Tibet. He built phodrang karpo (White Palace) to the east and west of the Hall of Avalokitesvara which had remained from King Songtsan Gambo's time. The construction lasted eight years. In 1653 the fifth Dalai Lama returned from Beijing where he had had an audience with Emperor Shun Zhi (reigned from 1643 to 1661) and, very pleased with the White Palace, decided to move his residence and office from Drepung Monastery to it.

The Red Palace was built between 1690 and 1693 in memory of the fifth Dalai Lama. It makes up the central part of the complex and is surrounded by the buildings of the White Palace. A hall was specially built to keep the salt-dried and embalmed remains of the fifth Dalai Lama who had died eight years earlier.

A recommended route for visitors to the Potala Palace starts at the eastern gate. Through the four-meter-long gateway one comes to the 1,600-square-meter Deyangxia Terrace. Here, celebrations are held on holidays or religious occasions, with songs and dances. A stairway leads from there to various parts of the entire palace. The walls of the stairway are covered with murals. Those on the eastern wall depict a sketch map of Chang'an (present-day Xi'an, then

11

capital of the Tang Dynasty) and the Tang Emperor testing the wisdom of the Tibetan envoy who came to ask for the hand of a Tang princess for King Songtsan Gambo. Those on the northern wall describe the scenes of Princess Wenchang on her way to marry King Songtsan Gambo in Lhasa.

Further along the stairway is the East Main Hall. The largest building of the White Palace was built in 1645. Its oversized roof is supported by 48 thick wooden columns. The poor light adds more solemnity and mystery to the immense interior. In 1653 Emperor Shun Zhi conferred the formal title on the fifth Dalai Lama and sent to him a gold seal and mandate. After that ceremonies for the assumption of office by the Dalai Lamas were presided over in this hall by ministers from the Qing court in Beijing. Major religious and political activities also took place here.

The Dalai Lama's living chambers, called the East and West Sunlight Halls, were at the crest of the White Palace. These include prayer halls, halls housing Buddhist sutras, sitting rooms and bedrooms, all luxuriously furnished and decorated with jewels and other treasures. The Dalai Lama chanted scriptures, held morning court and received high-ranking lamas in the West Sunlight Hall. In his leisure time he would take a walk on the spacious platform outside the Sunlight Halls, admiring the mountains in distance and watching the crowds in Lhasa city.

The Red Palace contains mainly prayer halls and eight stupas (dome-like mounds) in which the embalmed bodies of the dead Dalai Lamas rest in a meditation position. The tops of the stupas are covered with gilded copper tiles and decorated with gold leaf and precious stones. The stupa of the fifth Dalai Lama is the oldest and the largest. The last one is for the 13th Dalai Lama (1876-1933). The largest hall of the Red Palace is devoted to the fifth Dalai Lama. A pair of embroidered curtains in the hall were a present to the fifth Dalai Lama from Emperor Kang Xi (reigned from 1661 to 1722). The emperor ordered a workshop built to make these curtains in one year. When a new Dalai Lama assumed the office, these curtains would be hung up in a con-

spicuous place in the hall.

The stupa with the remains of the fifth Dalai Lama is 14.85 meters high, covered with gold leaf and studded with pearls, jadeite, agate and precious stones. Its construction used 3,721 kilograms of gold and 32,557 kilograms of silver. Beside the body of the fifth Dalai Lama the stupa also contains 19,180 kilograms of barley and wheat, and large quantities of butter, tea, sandalwood, precious stones, silk and Buddhist scriptures.

Built between 1934 and 1936 the three-story Stupa Hall of the 13th Dalai Lama is located to the western end of the Red Palace. The walls on the top floor are covered with murals depicting episodes of the 13th Dalai Lama's life. The stupa, 14 meters high, is covered with gold leaf and decorated with precious stones like other stupas. One can enter the stupa through an opening in the front side, known as "Eyesight Door". A latticed screen divides the interior of the stupa into two parts. An image of the Eleven-Faced Avalokitesvara with Thousand Arms and Thousand Eyes is worshipped in a niche in the front part. A Buddha bed in the rear part is equipped with a canopy, curtains, quilts and pillows. A wooden chest on the bed contains the body of the 13th Dalai Lama. On a desk in front of the bed are musical instruments, Buddhist scriptures, an ink bottle and bamboo writing brushes, used by the 13th Dalai Lama. An exquisite *mandala* (a Buddhist ornamental object) by the stupa is made with more than 200,000 pearls and coral beads strung together. A four-tiered framework in the center of the *mandala* is topped with a gold tower which keeps a statue of the 13th Dalai Lama. The statue was cast with 31 kilograms of silver. The tassels around the gold tower are strings of pearls and coral beads.

Up to the second floor from the West Main Hall one enters a gallery. The paintings on the walls describe the construction scenes of the Red Palace. Further ahead is the cave-dwelling where King Songtsan Gambo read Buddhist scriptures. The 1,300-year-old room keeps the statues of King Songtsan Gambo, Princess Wencheng, Princess Bhrikuti (Chi Zun) of Nepal (the king's another wife) and court officials. The Hall of Avalokitesvara above King Songtsan Gambo's cave-dwelling is the oldest building of the Potala Palace. It is said Songtsan Gambo was an incarnation of this bodhisattva. The fifth Dalai Lama read Buddhist scriptures in this hall. Eight Buddha statues of sandalwood, a present from Emperor Shun Zhi to the fifth Dalai Lama, are displayed in this hall.

The Trilokya Hall, built in 1679, is the highest building of the Red Palace and the center of the whole Potala Palace. A memorial tablet inscribed with the title of Emperor Kang Xi in this hall was brought from Beijing by the seventh Dalai Lama (1708-1757). This hall also has a portrait of Emperor Qian Long (reigned 1735-1795) brought from Beijing by the eighth Dalai Lama (1758-1804).

The Potala Palace is a sacred site of Tibetan Buddhist followers and a treasure of architecture in China. It is a perfect combination of an imperial palace and a Buddhist monastery to meet the needs of the ancient rule in Tibet where the Dalai Lama was in charge both of the religious and civil affairs. The imposing complex evokes respect for the awesome power of the Buddha. Inside the different quarters housed all the functional organs of a government and provided living and work places for government officials and lamas.

The palace stone foundations are laid deep into the Red Mountain as if the buildings grew out of the solid rock. The outer wall, several meters thick, had copper poured into its interstices to give it strength and resistance to earthquakes. The upper structure of the palace is of wood. Spaces are left between the wooden structure and the stone walls to serve as an insulating layer. Since many construction workers came from central China, Mongolia and Nepal, their ethnical features can be seen in the layout, exterior and interior decorations and paintings.

The Potala Palace houses a large amount of cultural relics and jewelry. The number of Buddhist statues of gold, jade, bronze, wood and stone comes to more than 10,000. There are numerous Buddhist portraits. The murals, outstanding as works of art, were done by Tibetan artists in the 17th century. Some are on religious themes, others show the life of the Tibetan people at the time. No one has ever counted how many murals in the palace. But a corridor on the second floor of the Red Palace alone contains 698 sections.

The Potala Palace also houses a large number of early copies of Buddhist sutras in Sanskrit, including a copy with the words pricked out on palm leaves by needles. It is the earliest Buddhist scripture brought from India to Tibet. The "Ganzhur" sutra was written in gold powder. Another sutra, "Danzhur" of more than 100 volumes, was written in a mixture of ground gold, silver, coral and sea shells. The Potala Palace also keeps the jade seals and mandates conferred on the Tibetan aristocrats by the central government after the Yuan Dynasty (1206-1368), and many valuable musical instruments, prayer banners, Tibetan carpets and curtains.

The Chinese government pays great attention to the preservation of the Potala Palace. In 1961 the State Council placed the palace on the list of cultural sites to be accorded special protection. It also set up a research group to sort out and study the vast number of objects stored there and a special fund for its repair. In 1988 the central government decided to carry out an overall renovation of the Potala Palace. A team of specialists formulated a plan after three months of intensive study. The giant project began in October 1989. Workers and artisans, mainly Tibetans, finished the 77 renovation items on 28,000 square meters in more than three years. The walls were reinforced with cracks sealed up; rotten pillars, beams and rafters were replaced; murals were cleaned to show their original bright colors; and fire hazards were eliminated. Over the three years of work, no single object in the Potala Palace was damaged or missing. The workers did a wonderful job when they reinforced the Stupa Hall of the fifth Dalai Lama—they did not remove any pillar or beam of the roof, thus retaining the original state of the structure. Now this grand edifice of the Potala Palace looks even brighter under the blue sky on the Tibet Plateau.

历世达赖喇嘛世系表

世　次	名　字	生　卒　年
一世	根敦珠巴	(1391－1474)
二世	根敦嘉措	(1475－1542)
三世	索南嘉措	(1543－1588)
四世	云丹嘉措	(1589－1616)
五世	罗桑嘉措	(1617－1682)
六世	仓央嘉措	(1683－1706)
七世	格桑嘉措	(1708－1757)
八世	强白嘉措	(1758－1804)
九世	隆朵嘉措	(1805－1815)
十世	楚臣嘉措	(1816－1837)
十一世	克珠嘉措	(1838－1855)
十二世	成烈嘉措	(1856－1875)
十三世	土登嘉措	(1876－1933)
十四世	丹增嘉措	(1934－　　)

Lineage of the Dalai Lamas

First Dalai Lama	Gedun Truppa	(1391-1474)
Second Dalai Lama	Gedun Gyatso	(1475-1542)
Third Dalai Lama	Sonam Gyatso	(1543-1588)
Fourth Dalai Lama	Yonten Gyatso	(1589-1616)
Fifth Dalai Lama	Lozang Gyatso	(1617-1682)
Sixth Dalai Lama	Tsangyang Gyatso	(1683-1706)
Seventh Dalai Lama	Kelzang Gyatso	(1708-1757)
Eighth Dalai Lama	Jampal Gyatso	(1758-1804)
Ninth Dalai Lama	Lungtok Gyatso	(1805-1815)
Tenth Dalai Lama	Tsutrim Gyatso	(1816-1837)
Eleventh Dalai Lama	Khedrup Gyatso	(1838-1855)
Twelveth Dalai Lama	Trinley Gyatso	(1856-1875)
Thirteenth Dalai Lama	Tupden Gyatso	(1876-1933)
Fourteenth Dalai Lama	Tenzin Gyatso	(1934-　　)

布达拉宫外景 布达拉宫耸立在海拔 3700 米的红山上，是世界上基址最高、规模最大的宫堡式建筑群。

The Potala Palace The palace rises on the south wall of the Red Mountain 3,700 meters above sea level, the only Buddhist site in the world at such a high altitude.

日光城中的宫堡

　　布达拉宫位于拉萨市内的红山上，占地 13 万平方米，始建于公元 7 世纪，17 世纪加以重修和扩建。历代曾有九位藏王、十位达赖喇嘛在此居住。主体建筑分白宫、红宫两大部分。宫内陈设豪华，有大量壁画、唐卡、佛雕和古玩珍宝，堪称西藏佛教文化博物馆。

Sacred Site in the 'City of Sunshine'

　　The Potala Palace on the Red Mountain in Lhasa occupies an area of 130,000 square meters. It was built in the seventh century and was reconstructed in the 17th century. Through its history of 1,300 years it was the residence and office of nine Tibetan kings and ten Dalai Lamas. The whole complex is divided into two parts: the White Palace and the Red Palace. The great museum of Tibetan Buddhist culture contains large quantities of murals, tangka portraits, Buddhist images and jewels.

侧视布达拉宫 宫堡依山势而筑，高低凹凸，纵横延伸，各个侧面均呈现出奇异雄伟的造型。

A side view of the Potala Palace The halls and chambers of the palace spread out along the hill face to give a diversed outlook from various angles.

仰视布达拉宫 从近处仰视，白色的宫墙与碧空交相辉映，愈显雄奇。

An upturned view of the Potala Palace At a close look upward the white palace walls seem to blend into the blue sky.

布达拉宫雪景　雪后的布达拉宫，富丽中透出清雅，别有情趣。

Snow over the Potala Palace　When the palace is covered in snow it gives another beautiful sight.

从大昭寺眺望布达拉宫　从山麓至宫堡顶部高达178米，不论置身于拉萨市哪个方位，都能望见它的雄姿。

Potala Palace seen from Jokhang Monastery　The 178-meter-high palace can be seen from every corner in Lhasa.

人间仙境 布达拉宫枕山临水，高耸入云，观之疑为人 ▶
间仙境。

Fairyland on earth The Potala Palace looks like a
fairyland with the Red Mountain behind and the Lhasa
River in front of it.

宫前阶道 阶道约有石阶 250 级，呈"Z"形曲折升高，直达宫门。

Stone stairs in front of the Potala Palace Stone stairs of 250 steps lead to the east gate of the palace.

宫堡檐下墙顶 外墙顶部周缘，采用染成绛红色的白玛草贴饰，这不仅是一种独特的建筑艺术，也是一种等级的象征。

The upper walls The upper walls of the Potala Palace are girdled with bundles of the stalks of a local plant dyed red to create the effect of a colorful sash.

宫堡外墙　用花岗岩垒砌，最厚处达 5 米，部份墙体夹层内还灌注铁汁，坚固异常。

The outer palace wall　The outer wall of granite blocks is five meters thick in some parts. Copper was poured into its interstices to give it strength.

檐下雕饰　白玛草上，镶嵌着金光熠熠的铜质鎏金法轮、瑞兽和其他吉祥图案，既显高贵，又有宗教气息。

Ornaments on the upper walls　Gilded bronze Dharma (Law) Wheel, animals of auspice and other designs are hung on the stalk bundles on the upper walls to enhance the religious atmosphere.

檐下雕饰

Ornaments on the upper walls.

西宫门 布达拉宫设有东、南、西三门，南门为正门，东、西二门位于后山，是后门。图为西门外诵经的佛教信徒。

West Palace Gate The Potala Palace has three entrances. The south gate is the main entrance. The east and west gates are located behind the hill. The picture shows Buddhist followers chanting scriptures at the west gate.

后山道 红山北坡，辟有登山的便道和马道，行人、车辆由此可以直抵布达拉宫后门。

Mountain paths There are paths on the north side of the Red Mountain. People can reach the rear gate of the Potala Palace either on foot or by carriages.

朝圣者 布达拉宫是历世达赖喇嘛居住的城堡，被佛教信徒视为圣地，朝拜者络绎不绝。

Pilgrims Buddhist followers come to the Potala Palace in a constant flow all year round to pay their respect to the holy place.

龙王潭 为布达拉宫后园，位于红山北麓，原是达赖喇嘛游赏的园林，现为拉萨市公园之一。园内林幽草碧，碧波荡漾，风景宜人。

Dragon King Pool The Dragon King Pool on the north side of the Red Mountain was a garden for the Dalai Lamas. Now it is a public park. The clear water and luxuriant trees make a pleasant sight.

龙王潭古柳
Ancient willow trees by the Dragon King Pool.

布达拉宫入口 位于"Z"形磴道尽头，坐西面东。

Entrance to the Potala Palace Visitors usually enter the Potala Palace from the east gate.

德阳厦 为正门内一面积达 1600 平方米的广阔平台，每逢宗教喜庆节日，在此举行跳神活动。

Deyangxia Terrace The 1,600-square-meter platform is located at the east gate. Holiday celebrations and major religious activities are held here.

圆堡　白宫外围建有四座圆堡，用于防卫。图为东侧圆堡。

Circular Castles　Four circular towers stand on the outer wall as guardhouses. The picture shows one on the east side.

白　宫

位于宫堡东部，是达赖喇嘛的冬宫，也曾是原西藏地方政府办事机构所在地，高七层。位于第四层中央的东有寂圆满大殿，是举行达赖喇嘛坐床、亲政等重大典仪活动的场所。第五、六层是摄政办公和生活用房。最高一层有两套达赖喇嘛冬季的起居宫。由于这里终日阳光普照，故称东、西日光殿。

The White Palace

The seven-story White Palace, the eastern part of the Potala, was the winter residence of the Dalai Lamas and the local government office. The East Main Hall on the fourth floor was used for the ceremonies for the assumption of office by the Dalai Lamas. The fifth and sixth floors were offices and living quarters of the Tibetan government. Two groups of buildings on the top floor were winter residence of the Dalai Lama. The buildings are sunny so are named Sunlight Halls.

白宫外景

The White Palace.

白宫门廊　又名达松格廊道，它是通往宫内各殿堂的必经之路。门廊梁柱雕有菩萨、法器、缠枝花卉等具有佛教特色的图案。

Gate corridor of the White Palace　The corridor from the main entrance leads to every hall and chamber in the White Palace. The beams and pillars of it are carved with designs on Buddhist themes and plants.

五世达赖喇嘛手印模　位于门廊南壁一玻璃罩内。这是17世纪中期修建布达拉宫时留下的印记。当时，五世达赖喇嘛年事已高，一切政事均委以第巴桑结加措管理，而第巴威望不高，难以服众，故按朱砂手印为记，以当命令。图中手印之上即为晓谕僧俗的文告。

Hand prints of the fifth Dalai Lama　When the reconstruction of the Potala Palace was under way the fifth Dalai Lama was too old to supervise the project personally. He put his hand print on the decrees so his chief administor Sangye Gynatso could implement them on his behalf. The decrees with his hand prints are kept in a glass case on the wall of the gate corridor of the White Palace.

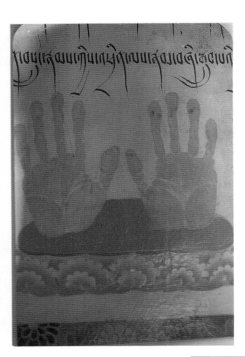

门廊壁画　达松格廊道四壁均绘有壁画。图中壁画描绘
7 世纪时布达拉宫落成，人们载歌载舞庆贺的情景。

Murals on the gate corridor　The paintings on the
walls of the gate corridor record the celebrations of
the completion of the Potala Palace in the seventh
century.

五难婚使图 绘于廊道东壁，描绘公元634年吐蕃使者禄东赞（？～667年）奉命到长安向唐王朝（618～907年）请求联姻，连克五道难题，终于不辱使命的情景。

Five Riddles for The Tibetan Envoy In 634 an envoy was sent by Songtsan Gambo, King of Tubo, to ask for the hand of a princess of the Tang Dynasty (618-907). When he arrived at the court he was given five riddles to answer. He succeeded and the Tang emperor agreed to marry Princess Wencheng to the Tibetan king.

◀ ▼ **文成公主进藏图** 绘于廊道北壁，描绘文成公主一行由
长安至拉萨的沿途情景，以及抵达拉萨时受到热烈欢迎
的场面。此图为"文成公主进藏图"局部。

'Princess Wencheng on Her Way to Tibet' The
painting on the north wall of the gate corridor depicts
the scenes on the road when Princess Wencheng trav-
eled from Tang capital Chang'an to Lhasa to marry
King Songtsan Gambo and the jubilant crowds receiv-
ing her.

白宫大门　位于门廊内。进入此门，便是白宫主殿东有
寂圆满大殿。

The front gate of the White Palace　Behind the gate
is the East Main Hall of the White Palace.

大殿匾额　东有寂圆满大殿，简称东大殿，是历世达赖喇嘛举行坐床、亲政大典及重大宗教活动的场所。面积717平方米，是白宫最大的殿堂。图为大殿北侧上方所悬清同治皇帝（1861～1874年在位）所书的"振锡绥疆"匾额。

Plaque in the East Main Hall　Celebrations for the assumption of office by the Dalai Lamas and major religious and civil activities took place in the East Main Hall. The largest building of the White Palace has a floor space of 717 square meters. The characters inscribed on the plaque near the north wall are in the handwriting of Emperor Tong Zhi (reigned between 1861 and 1874) of the Qing Dynasty.

西日光殿　是早期修筑的达赖喇嘛起居宫，位于白宫顶层。由福地妙旋宫、福足欲聚宫、喜足绝顶宫、寝宫和护法殿组成。图为福足欲聚宫。

West Sunlight Hall　This hall is the highest building of the White Palace and composed of several chambers serving as the living quarters of the Dalai Lama. The picture shows one of the chambers: the Happiness Gathering Palace.

喜足绝顶宫内景

Supreme Happiness Palace　It is one of the chambers of the West Sunlight Hall.

喜足绝顶宫内佛龛

Buddha niche in the Supreme Happiness Palace.

喜足光明宫内佛龛

Inside the Bright Happiness Palace.

东日光殿 是十三世达赖喇嘛晚年增建的起居宫，由喜足光明宫、永固福德宫、护法殿、长寿尊胜宫和寝宫组成，内部设置与西日光殿大致相同。图为喜足光明宫。

East Sunlight Hall This hall was built as the living quarters of the 13th Dalai Lama. Like the West Sunlight Hall it is also composed of several chambers and has similar decorations. The picture shows one of the chambers—the Bright Happiness Palace.

永固福德宫 宫内陈设达赖喇嘛宝座，其上悬挂上师供养资粮田唐卡。

Everlasting Happiness and Virtue Palace This chamber of the East Sunlight Hall keeps a throne of the Dalai Lama. Hanging above the throne is a tangka picture with portraits of Super Masters.

达赖喇嘛宝座　图中宝座置于护法殿内。宝座靠背上双龙捧一法轮，象征着达赖喇嘛乃是佛界至高无上的尊者。

Throne of the Dalai Lama　The back of the throne is decorated with two dragons holding up the Dharma Wheel, symbolizing the supreme power of the Dalai Lama.

日光殿外阳台　在台上凭栏远眺，远山近水一览无余。

Platform outside the Sunlight Halls　From this vantage point one has a grand view of the mountains and the Lhasa River around Lhasa.

红宫外景　The Red Palace.

红宫灵塔殿

红宫，主要是达赖喇嘛的灵塔殿和各类佛殿。灵塔殿共有八座，用于供奉存放各世达赖喇嘛法体的灵塔，其中以五世和十三世达赖喇嘛灵塔殿最为壮观。西有寂圆满大殿是五世达赖喇嘛的享堂，也是布达拉宫最大的殿堂，内壁满绘壁画，极具历史文化价值。

红宫建于 1690 年，当时清康熙皇帝特派 114 名汉、满族工匠协同修建。

Stupas in the Red Palace

The Red Palace mainly composed of stupas and prayer halls. The eight stupas (dome-like mounds) keep the salted and embalmed bodies of the dead Dalai Lamas. Those of the fifth Dalai Lama and the 13th Dalai Lama are the most imposing. The West Main Hall, the largest building of the Potala Palace, is devoted to the fifth Dalai Lama. It contains many murals of high historic and artistic value.

Construction of the Red Palace began in 1690. Emperor Kang Xi of the Qing Dynasty sent 114 Han and Manchu artisans from Beijing to help with the project.

无字碑　1693 年 4 月，红宫主体建筑竣工，举行隆重的开光大典，并在宫前立无字石碑，以示纪念。

Wordless Stele　The Red Palace was completed in April 1693. The memorial stele was erected in front of it to mark the occasion.

金顶区 金顶指的是灵塔殿和主供佛殿的鎏金铜顶,有歇山、六角亭等形式,共七座,集中于宫堡最顶端。

Golden Tops Seven stupa and prayer halls of the Red Palace have gabled or hexagonal roofs covered with gilded copper tiles. They are the highest buildings of the Potala Palace.

金顶 金顶及其装饰融汇了中国汉族地区和印度、尼泊尔等国的建筑风格，是文化交流的产物。

Gabled Roof The gabled roof is of typical architectural style of central China. But the decorations show the influence of India and Nepal.

金顶飞檐上的神鲸

Divine whale on an upturned eave.

金顶上的共命鸟

Fate-Sharing Bird on the Golden Tops.

金顶上的法幢
Prayer bell on the Golden Tops.

西有寂圆满大殿　简称西大殿，是五世达赖喇嘛的享堂。面积 725 平方米，是布达拉宫最大的殿堂。有门与世袭、菩提道次第、持明等殿相通。

West Main Hall　The largest prayer hall devoted to the fifth Dalai Lama has a floor space of 725 square meters. Through its gates one can go to several other halls.

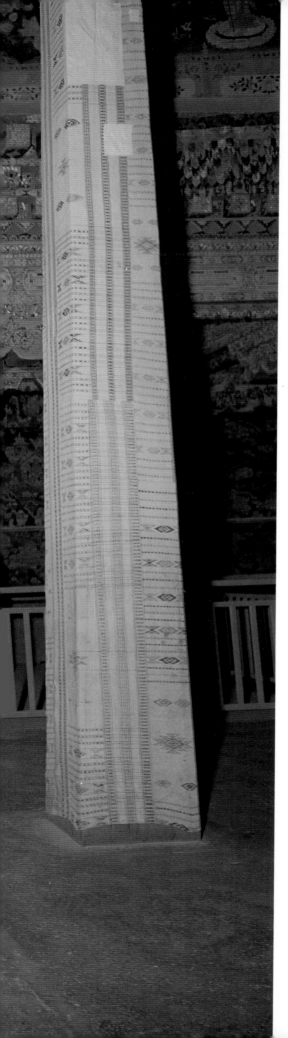

西大殿梁枋彩雕

Colored carvings on the pillars of the
West Main Hall.

达赖喇嘛宝座　位于西大殿中央，其上高悬清乾隆皇帝
1760年所书"涌莲初地"匾额。

Throne of the Dalai Lama　The throne is placed in
the middle of the West Main Hall. Hanging above the
throne is a plaque with an inscription written by Emperor Qian Long in 1760.

57

五世达赖喇嘛觐见清顺治皇帝图 西大殿四壁绘有记录五世达赖喇嘛生平业迹的壁画，面积达 280 余平方米，尤以东壁一组最为详尽，描绘了 1652 年五世达赖喇嘛进京觐见清顺治皇帝的情景。

'The Fifth Dalai Lama Meets with Emperor Shun Zhi' Paintings of 280 square meters on the walls of the West Main Hall describe the life of the fifth Dalai Lama. Those on the east wall show a scene when Emperor Shu Zhi of the Qing Dynasty gave an audience to the fifth Dalai Lama in Beijing in 1652.

五世达赖喇嘛灵塔殿大门

Front gate of the Stupa Hall of the fifth Dalai
Lama.

五世达赖喇嘛灵塔殿 位于西大殿以西，殿内中央置五世达赖喇嘛灵塔。另有十世、十二世达赖喇嘛灵塔和八座镶有各种珍宝的银质善逝佛塔陈于殿中。

Stupa Hall of the fifth Dalai Lama The hall housing the stupa with the remains of the fifth Dalai Lama is located to the west of the West Main Hall. The hall also houses the stupas of the 10th and 12th Dalai Lamas and eight Buddhist pagodas decorated with precious stone and silver objects.

五世达赖喇嘛灵塔　塔高 14.85 米，塔身用金箔包裹，耗黄金 3721 公斤，塔面镶嵌珠宝上万颗，是一件使用综合工艺、做工高超的艺术珍品。塔内保存着五世达赖喇嘛的遗骸。

Stupa of the fifth Dalai Lama　The pagoda-shaped stupa is 14.85 meters high and studded with more than 10,000 pearls and precious stones. The gold leaf is made with 3,721 kilograms of gold. It keeps the remains of the fifth Dalai Lama.

世袭殿内景 殿内正中并列供奉金质释迦牟尼（约前565～前486年）、银质五世达赖喇嘛坐像；右侧供有一至四世达赖喇嘛坐像；邻西墙置有十一世达赖喇嘛的灵塔和坐像。

Inside the Inheritance Hall A gold statue of Sakyamuni (c. 565-486 B. C.), and a silver statue of the fifth Dalai Lama are placed in the middle of the Inheritance Hall. On their right there are the seated statues from the first to the fourth Dalai Lamas, and near the west wall there is the stupa containing the remains of the 11th Dalai Lama and a seated statue of him.

世袭殿 位于西大殿以北，殿门上方悬有清乾隆皇帝题赐的"大悲超宗"匾额。

Inheritance Hall The hall to the north of the West Main Hall preserves a plaque with an inscription written by Emperor Qian Long of the Qing Dynasty.

释迦牟尼和五世达赖喇嘛坐像　释迦牟尼，姓乔达摩，
名悉达多，佛教创始人。五世达赖喇嘛，本名阿旺罗桑
嘉措，藏传佛教格鲁派（黄教）首领，对达赖喇嘛系统
在西藏政教地位的确立做出了杰出贡献。

**Seated statues of Sakyamuni and the fifth Dalai
Lama**　Sakyamuni is the founder of Buddhism.
Lozang Gyatso, the fifth Dalai Lama, was leader of
the Gelupas (Yellow) Sect who was crucial for the es-
tablishment of Buddhism in Tibet.

十一世达赖喇嘛坐像　十一世达赖喇嘛（1838－1855年），本名克珠嘉措，经金瓶掣签被选为十一世达赖喇嘛。1855年清政府令其亲政，不幸于当年亡故。

Seated statue of the 11th Dalai Lama　Khedrup Gyantso (1838-1855), the 11th Dalai Lama, was confirmed by the central government of the Qing Dynasty in 1855. But he died in the same year.

十一世达赖喇嘛灵塔　塔内存十一世达赖喇嘛遗骸。

Stupa of the 11th Dalai Lama　It contains the remains of the 11th Dalai Lama.

一世达赖喇嘛像 一世达赖喇嘛（1391~1474 年），本名根敦珠巴，是黄教创始人宗喀巴大师（1357~1419）的大弟子之一，后藏扎什伦布寺的创建者，1578 年被追认为第一世达赖喇嘛。

Statue of the first Dalai Lama Gedun Truppa was a disciple of Zongkaba (1357-1419), the founder of the Yellow Sect. He built the Zashilunbu Monastery in Xigaze and, in 1578, was posthumously declared the first Dalai Lama.

二世达赖喇嘛像 二世达赖喇嘛（1475~1542 年），本名根敦嘉措，1578 年被追认为第二世达赖喇嘛。

Statue of the second Dalai Lama Gendun Gyatso (1475-1542) was post humously made the second Dalai Lama in 1578.

三世达赖喇嘛像　三世达赖喇嘛（1543～1588 年），本名索南嘉措，1578 年受蒙古土默特部首领俺答汗所封"圣识一切瓦齐尔达喇达赖喇嘛"尊号，这是"达赖喇嘛"称号的起始。

Statue of the third Dalai Lama In 1578 Altan Khan of the Mongols conferred the title of Dalai Lama on Sonam Gyatso（1543-1588）. The title of the Dalai Lama thus began to be formally used in Tibet.

四世达赖喇嘛像　四世达赖喇嘛（1589～1616 年），本名云丹嘉措，蒙古土默特部人，俺答汗之曾孙，1602 年被确认为达赖喇嘛灵童，迎请入藏。

Statue of the fourth Dalai Lama Yonten Gyatso (1589-1616), the fourth Dalai Lama, was the great-grandson of Altan Khan of the Mongols. He was first identified by native Mongols as the soul boy and was brought to Tibet in 1602.

宗喀巴像 供奉于菩提道次第殿，此殿位于西大殿东侧。宗喀巴为黄教祖师，其塑像两边及正前方另有七十余尊格鲁派、噶当派高僧造像陪供。

Statue of Zongkaba A statue of Zongkaba, founder of the Yellow Sect, is worshipped in the Bodhi Cultivation Hall to the east of the West Main Hall. Flanking it are statues of high lamas.

持明殿　位于西大殿南侧，殿内主供莲花生银铸坐像。莲花生系印度高僧，公元 8 世纪中叶应吐蕃赞普赤松德赞（754～797 年在位）之请入藏传播佛教，被后世藏传佛教宁玛派（红教）尊为"祖师"。

Light-Holding Hall　A seated statue of Padmasambhava, Great Tantric Master from India, is worshipped in this hall. The Indian monk came at the invitation of Tibetan king to propagate Buddhism in the mid-eighth century. His followers became known later as the Nying-ma-pa (Red) Sect.

菩提道次第殿中的银铸善逝佛塔

Silver pagoda in the Bodhi Cultivation Hall.

莲花生祖师传承像 持明殿东侧供有八尊莲花生祖师传
承铜像，此为其一。

Statues of Padmasambhava There are eight statues
of the Great Tantric Master in the Light-Holding
Hall. The picture shows one of them.

莲花生祖师传承造像

Statue of Padmasambhava.

莲花生祖师传承造像

Statue of Padmasambhava.

莲花生祖师传承造像

Statue of Padmasambhava.

莲花生祖师变身像
A changed form of Padmasambhava.

莲花生祖师变身像 持明殿西侧为八尊莲花生祖师变身像，图为其一。

Changed forms of Padmasambhava Along the west wall of the Light-Holding Hall there are eight statues of the changed forms of Padmasambhava. The picture shows one of them.

莲花生祖师变身像　　A changed form of Padmasambhava.

莲花生祖师变身像   A changed form of Padmasambhava.

持明殿内造像

Statues in the Light-Holding Hall.

经书架　图中经书架位于持明殿内，架上存放着用藏、汉、满、蒙四种文字精刻的《甘珠尔》经。《甘珠尔》意为佛语部，编成于 14 世纪后半叶，共收书 1108 种，是释迦牟尼生前讲授的佛教经典。

Shelves with Buddhist scriptures　The shelves in the Light-Holding Hall keep the "Ganzhur" sutra in the Tibetan, Chinese, Manchurian and Mongolian script. The sutra has collected in 1,108 volumes of the teachings of Sakyamuni.

七世达赖喇嘛灵塔殿 殿中央供奉七世达赖喇嘛格桑嘉措的灵塔，殿内尚有七世达赖喇嘛坐像，以及佛龛、经书架等。

Stupa Hall of the seventh Dalai Lama The stupa containing the remains of Kelzang Gyatso, the seventh Dalai Lama, is placed in the center. In this hall there is also a seated statue of the seventh Dalai Lama and Buddha niches and shelves with Buddhist scriptures.

六世达赖喇嘛坐像 六世达赖喇嘛（1683～1706 年），本名仓央嘉措，是一位诗人，1705 年被废，在被执送京师（北京）途中病逝。此像供于上师殿。

Seated statue of the sixth Dalai Lama Tsangyang Gyatso（1683-1706），the sixth Dalai Lama, was a poet and much loved by the Tibetans. But he was stripped of the title in 1705 and died on the road to Beijing where he was being brought for punishment. His statue is worshipped in the Master Hall.

灵塔殿门廊上的壁画（局部）　　Mural (detail) on the gate corridor of the Stupa Hall.

壁画局部　　Mural（detail）．▶

金刚力士造像　塑于七世达赖喇嘛灵塔前，其形英武勇
猛。

Statue of Vajra（Buddha's warrior attendant）in
front of the stupa of the seventh Dalai Lama.

八世达赖喇嘛坐像　八世达赖喇嘛，本名强白嘉措，1781 年清政府令其亲政，与中央政府合作友善。图中坐像供于八世达赖喇嘛灵塔殿内。

Seated statue of the eighth Dalai Lama Jampal Gyatso, the eighth Dalai Lama, was confirmed by the Qing court in 1781. He was on very good terms with the central government. The statue is housed in the Stupa Hall of the eighth Dalai Lama.

供物　八世达赖喇嘛灵塔前供奉有八瑞物、八吉祥徽、七政宝等。图为八吉祥徽之一。

Sacrificial pieces Sacrificial pieces in front of the stupa of the eighth Dalai Lama include the "Eight Auspicious Objects, Eight Lucky Emblems and Seven Treasures". The picture shows one of the "Eight Lucky Emblems".

九世达赖喇嘛灵塔殿大门

Front gate of the Stupa Hall of the ninth Dala
Lama.

九世达赖喇嘛像　九世达赖喇嘛（1805～1815 年），法名隆朵嘉措，1808 年清政府批准他免于金瓶掣签，启用前辈达赖喇嘛之印，可惜年仅十一岁便夭亡。此像供于九世达赖喇嘛灵塔殿内。

Statue of the ninth Dalai Lama　Lungtok Gyatso (1805-1815), was confirmed by the Qing court as the ninth Dalai Lama in 1808. But he died at the age of 11. His statue is housed in his stupa hall.

十三世达赖喇嘛灵塔　供于十三世达赖喇嘛灵塔殿内，于 1933 年动工，历时三年建成。塔高约 14 米，塔面用黄金包裹，镶珠嵌玉，甚是珍奇。

Stupa of the 13th Dalai Lama　Construction of the stupa began in 1933 and completed in three years. The 14-meter-high structure is covered with gold leaf and decorated with pearls and precious stones.

十三世达赖喇嘛像　供于十三世达赖喇嘛灵塔殿内。十三世达赖喇嘛，法名土登嘉措，执掌西藏政教两权达三十八年之久。

Statue of the 13th Dalai Lama　Tupden Gyatso, the 13th Dalai Lama, held the religious and civil power in Tibet for 38 years.

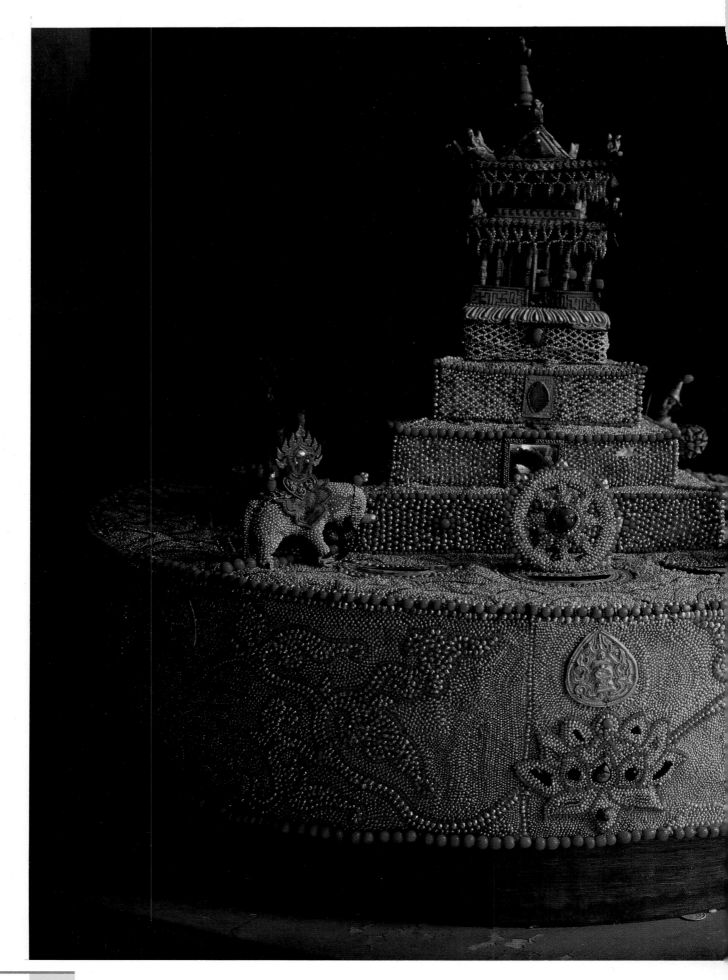

珍珠曼陀罗 置于十三世达赖喇嘛灵塔殿内，是由 20 万颗珍珠串成的稀世之宝。

Mandala *Mandala* in Sanskrit means Buddha Teaching Terrace. But later it became a pure ornamental object. This *mandala* is made with 200,000 pearls strung together.

十三世达赖喇嘛灵塔殿内佛龛

Buddha Niche in the Stupa Hall of the 13th Dalai
Lama.

十三世达赖喇嘛传略壁画 绘于其灵塔殿第三层四壁，北壁居中绘有十一面观音像。图为壁画局部。

Murals on the life of the 13th Dalai Lama Those murals are found on the walls of the third floor of the Stupa Hall of the 13th Dalai Lama. In the middle of the north wall is an image of the Eleven-Faced Bodhisattva. The picture shows a part of a mural.

法器、祭器 图中器物系十三世达赖喇嘛灵塔前的供品，多为清政府所赐。

Service and sacrificial pieces Many of the objects in front of the stupa of the 13th Dalai Lama were presents from the Qing court.

十三世达赖喇嘛进京觐见图　绘于十一面观音像周围，内容描绘 1908 年十三世
达赖喇嘛进京朝拜光绪皇帝（1874～1908 年在位）及慈禧太后（1835～1908
年）的情景。

'The 13th Dalai Lama at the Court in Beijing'　The murals around the
Eleven-Faced Bohisattva describe the 13th Dalai Lama meeting with Emperor
Guang Xu（reigned between 1874 and 1908）and Empress Dowager Ci Xi
（1835-1908）in 1908.

十一面观音像

Eleven-Faced Bodhisattva (Ekadasamukharalokitesvara).

布达拉宫僧人　各灵塔殿内，每天早晚均有僧人焚香、燃灯，终日香火不断。

Lamas in the Potala Palace　Lamas keep the incense sticks and lights burning all day long.

长寿乐集殿 殿中设六世达赖喇嘛宝座，沿墙佛龛中供奉千余尊无量寿佛、"埃革则底"护法神和宗喀巴塑像等两千余尊佛像。图为无量寿佛之一。

Longevity and Happiness Hall A throne for the sixth Dalai Lama is placed in the middle. More than 1,000 statues of Amitayus Buddha and 2,000 statues of Law Guardians and Master Zongkaba are in niches along the walls. The picture shows a statue of Amitayus.

红宫佛殿

　　作为佛教圣地，佛殿在布达拉宫占有重要地位，它们集中在红宫。其中法王洞等部分建筑是吐蕃时期遗存的布达拉宫最早的建筑物。殊胜三界殿是红宫最高的殿堂。此外还有无量寿佛殿、长寿乐集殿、弥勒佛殿、时轮殿、释迦能仁殿、菩提道次第殿、持明殿、世袭殿等等。

Prayer Halls in the Red Palace

As a Buddhist sanctuary the prayer Halls take an important place in the Potala Palace. The Dharma King Cave where King Songtsan Gambo once read Buddhist scriptures is the oldest structure of the Potala Palace. The Trilokya Hall is the highest building of the Red Palace. Other prayer halls include the Amitayus Hall, Longevity and Happiness Hall, Maitreya Hall, Kala Wheel Hall, Sakyamuni Hall, Bodhi Cultivation Hall, Light-Holding Hall and Inheritance Hall.

三怙主坐像　供于长寿乐集殿，由左至右分别为文殊师利、观音菩萨和金刚手菩萨，他们代表智慧、慈悲和威力。

Seated statues of Three Bodhisattvas　Manjursri, Avalokitesvara and Vajrapani (from left to right) in the Hall of Longevity and Happiness are representatives of wisdom, mercy and strength.

无量寿佛像　供于无量寿佛殿正面佛座上，共九尊。此佛即阿弥陀佛，为西方极乐世界现在佛。

Statues of Amitayu　Nine statues of Amitayu Buddha are placed on a dais in the Hall of Amitayu, the Present Buddha of the West Land of Supreme Happiness. ▶

白度母铜像　供于无量寿佛殿中。无量寿佛、白度母、
尊胜佛母是藏传佛教所奉"长寿三尊"。

Bronze statue of White Holy Mother　The statue is
worshipped in the Hall of Amitayu. Amitayu, White
Holy Mother and Arya Buddha Mother are the "Three
Sages of Longevity" in Tibetan Buddhism.

绿度母像 供于无量寿佛殿内。 度母，藏传佛教所奉佛母之一。传为观音化身，有救苦救难、济度众生的功德。现为二十一相，以白度母、绿度母较常见。

Green Holy Mother The statue is placed in the Hall of Amitayu. In Tibetan Buddhism the Holy Mother is the incarnation of the Goddess of Mercy who relieves sufferings of the world.

释迦能仁殿 殿中主供佛教始祖释迦牟尼像，图为大殿一隅。

Hall of Sakyamuni A statue of Sakyamuni is worshipped in this hall. The picture shows a part of the hall.

释迦牟尼坐像　　Seated statue of Sakyamuni.

经书架 陈于释迦能仁殿内，架上存手抄《甘珠尔》
经。

Shelves with scriptures A set of the hand-copied
'Ganzhur' sutra is kept on the selves in the Hall of
Sakyamuni.

僧人在整理经书
Lamas sorting out Buddhist scriptures.

在佛堂上供的僧人

Lamas present offerings in a prayer hall.

僧人诵经的情景

Lamas chanting scriptures.

弥勒佛殿内景　殿中主供弥勒佛鎏金铜像。弥勒佛，也称未来佛，佛教谓其蒙释迦牟尼授记，将继承释迦而在人间成佛。

Inside the Hall of Maitreya　A gilded bronze statue of Maitreya Buddha is worshipped in this hall. Maitreya, the Future Buddha, was ordained by Sakyamuni to become a Buddha of the secular world.

时轮殿　又称坛城殿，内有铜质立体坛城三座。坛城，梵文译音曼陀罗，原是佛教徒修法时安置佛、菩萨像的坛场，后以立体模型或绘制平面图代替。

Hall of the Kala (Time) Wheel　The hall keeps three *mandala*. In early days a *mandala* was a terrace to keep Buddha images, but later became an ornamental object with designs on Budddhist themes.

时轮金刚造像　时轮金刚，为藏传佛教密宗五部金刚大法的本尊之一。

Statue of Kala Wheel Vajra　Kala Wheel Vajra is one of the five Buddha's warrior attendants and a chief god of the Supreme Yogacara sect of Tibetan Buddhism.

时轮金刚坛城　三坛城之一，置于时轮殿中心，其周围佛龛内有时轮金刚像和历算家造像百余尊。

Mandala of Kala Wheel Vajra　This *mandala* in the center of the Hall of the Kala Wheel is surrounded by niches with more than 100 statues of Kala Wheel Vajra and other deities.

密集金刚坛城 时轮殿三坛城之一。

Mandala of Miji Vajra It is one of the three *mandalas* in the Hall of the Kala Wheel.

画廊 红宫二楼回廊内绘有壁画 698 幅，有"画廊"之称，图为外景。

Gallery The walls of a winding corridor on the second floor of the Red Palace bear 598 murals.

红宫回廊壁画 内容描绘兴建红宫及红宫落成庆典的盛况，还有赛马、射箭、摔跤等反映藏族人民生活习俗的壁画。图为"红宫落成图"。

Murals in the winding corridor of the Red Palace
The murals depict scenes celebrating the completion of the Red Palace, and horse race, archery and wrestling. The picture shows the mural "Completion of the Red Palace".

红宫回廊壁画（局部）

Mural in the winding corridor of the Red Palace
(detail).

红宫回廊壁画（局部）

Mural in the winding corridor of the Red Palace
(detail).

红宫回廊壁画（局部）

Mural in the winding corridor of the Red Palace (detail).

红宫回廊壁画（局部）

Mural in the winding corridor of the Red Palace (detail).

红宫回廊壁画（局部）

Mural in the winding corridor of the Red Palace (detail).

红宫回廊壁画（局部）

Mural in the winding corridor of the Red Palace (detail).

红宫回廊壁画（局部）

Mural in the winding corridor of the Red Palace (detail).

法王洞 松赞干布被西藏佛教徒尊为"法王"，他曾在此洞修行，故名"法王洞"。洞建于公元 7 世纪吐蕃时期，是布达拉宫内最古老的建筑。洞内有松赞干布、文成公主、尺尊公主等人的塑像。图为法王洞内景。

King of Dharma Cave Songtsan Gambo is called the King of Dharma (Law) by Tibetans. He read Buddhist scriptures in this cave-dwelling in the seventh century. Now there are the statues of King Songtsan Gambo, his wives Princess Wenchang and Princess Bhrikuti (Chi Zun).

松赞干布塑像 松赞干布，吐蕃赞普。在位期间，他统一了西藏诸部，建立了奴隶制的吐蕃王朝。他在政治、经济、文化等方面实行开放政策，为佛教的传播创造了有利条件。

Statue of Songtsan Gambo Songtsan Gambo unified Tibet and founded the Tubo regime in the seventh century. His open policy made it possible for Buddhism to spread in Tibet.

尺尊公主塑像 尺尊公主，尼泊尔王盎输伐摩的女儿，公元 632 年嫁与松赞干布为妻，为推动吐蕃王朝佛教发展起了一定作用。

Statue of Princess Bhrikuti Princess Bhrikuti (Chi Zun) of Nepal was married to King Songtsan Gambo in A. D. 632. She played an important role in propagating Buddhism in Tibet.

文成公主塑像 文成公主，唐宗室女，641 年与松赞干布联姻，对吐蕃经济、文化发展，汉藏文化交流作出了杰出贡献。

Statue of Princess Wenching Princess Wencheng of the Tang Dynasty was married to King Songtsan Gambo in A. D. 641. She made valuable contributions to the development of the economy and culture in Tibet.

吞米·桑布扎塑像 供于法王洞内。吞米·桑布扎，吐蕃王朝大臣，相传是藏文的创造者。

Statue of Tumi Sangbuzha The statue is in the King of Dharma Cave. Tumi Sangbuzha, an official of Tubo regime, is said to be the inventor of Tibetan written language.

禄东赞塑像 供于法王洞内。禄东赞,吐蕃大臣,曾赴长安为松赞干布求婚,并迎护文成公主入蕃。

Statue of Ludongtsan   The statue is found in the King of Dharma Cave. Ludongtsan was the envoy to the Tang court to ask for the hand of Princess Wencheng and escorted her to Tibet.

自在观音像 自在观音，为松赞干布所依本尊。此像供于圣观音殿内，是布达拉宫镇宫之宝。

Statue of the Avalokitesrava It is said Songtsan Gambo was the incarnation of Avalokitesrava. The statue is kept in the Hall of Avalokitesrava.

圣观音殿 藏名帕巴拉康，位于法王洞上层，殿门上方悬挂清同治皇帝御书"福田妙果"匾额。殿内供有檀香木雕自在观音像，是布达拉宫最神圣的殿堂。

Hall of Avalokitesrava The most sacred hall of the Potala Palace is located above the King of Dharma Cave. A sandalwood statue of Avalokitesrava is worshipped in this hall. The hall also keeps a plaque with an inscription written by Emperor Tong Zhi of the Qing Dynasty.

殊胜三界殿 藏名萨松朗杰，位于红宫第八层南侧，殿正面供有清康熙皇帝牌位和乾隆皇帝佛妆画像唐卡。清代 (1644～1911年) 每年藏历新年，达赖喇嘛都要率领噶厦官员和三大寺喇嘛到此朝拜。当时许多重大的政教活动如金瓶掣签等也在此举行。

Trilokya Hall This hall on the eighth floor of the Red Palace keeps a memorial tablet with the title of Emperor Kang Xi of the Qing Dynasty and a portrait of Emperor Qian Long. During the Qing Dynasty (1644-1911), on every Tibetan New Year's Day, the Dalai Lama would lead his officials and high lamas from the three largest monasteries to pay respect to the tablet and the portrait. Some grand ceremonies such as the confirmation of the soul boy also took place here.

康熙皇帝牌位 系七世达赖喇嘛请来的长生牌位，其上用藏、汉、满、蒙四种文字镌刻"当今皇帝万岁万万岁"金字。

Memorial tablet for Emperor Kang Xi An inscription on the tablet written in Tibetan, Chinese, Manchurian and Mongolian script reads: "A long, long life to the emperor!"

十一面观音像 供奉于殊胜三界殿内，其头部分五层，上部两层各一面，下部三层各三面，共十一面，耗白银310多公斤，是十三世达赖喇嘛主持铸造的。

Eleven-Faced Bodhisattva Five heads grow above the shoulders one upon another. There are two heads in the middle part of the statue and three heads in the lower part, eleven heads altogether. Made during the period of the 13th Dalai Lama, the statue was cast with 310 kilograms of silver.

唐卡 是藏传佛教特有的一种绘画艺术，按质地和制作工艺可分为绘制唐卡、织物唐卡和印刷唐卡。布达拉宫各处皆悬挂唐卡，其数难以胜计，此为绿度母及其刹土画像唐卡。

Tangka portraits Tangka portraits are a unique art of the Tibetan Buddhism. Some are painted, some are embroidered and still some are woven. The picture shows a portrait of Green Holy Mother.

宫藏文物

三百余年来，布达拉宫收藏和保存了极为丰富的历史文物。其中有 5 万余平方米壁画、近千座佛塔、上万幅唐卡和贝叶经、《甘珠尔》经、《丹珠尔》经等珍贵经文典籍；明清两代皇帝封赐达赖喇嘛的金册、金印、玉印以及大量的金银品、玉器、锦缎绣品及珍宝古玩等，是一座世所罕有的文物宝库。

Cultural Relics

The Potala Palace has preserved a great number of cultural relics through the past 300 years. They include 50,000 square meters of murals, nearly 1,000 Buddhist pagodas, more than 10,000 tangka portraits, pattra sutras, the 'Ganzhur' sutra and 'Danzhur' sutra; it also keeps the golden albums, seals of gold and jade, gold, silver and jade ornaments, and silk products conferred on Tibetan nobles by the Ming and Qing emperors.

密集金刚像唐卡 密集金刚，亦称集密金刚，为藏传佛教密宗五部金刚大法的本尊。其他四本尊为大威德金刚、胜乐金刚、时轮金刚和喜金刚。

Miji Vajra tangka   It is one of the five chief Buddha's warrior attendants in Tibetan Buddhism. The other four are named the Vajra of Great Power and Virtue, the Vajra of Victory and Joy, the Vajra of Kala Wheel and the Vajra of Happiness.

白度母像唐卡 唐卡上度母的面部和身躯均用珍珠串缀
而成，其余部分用彩色绸料拼贴补绣，精致华美。

Portrait of White Holy Mother The face and body
of the image are made with pearls strung together.
The limbs are patchwork of colored silk.

金《甘珠尔》经　置于持明殿内，经文用金汁缮写，藏、汉、满、蒙四种文字并列。

'Ganzhur' sutra　The Buddhist scripture stored in the Light-holding Hall is written with gold powder in Tibetan, Chinese, Manchurian and Mongolian script.

金《甘珠尔》经　置于持明殿内，经文用金汁缮写，藏、汉、满、蒙四种文字并列。

鎏金"开花献佛"　置于殊胜三界殿中，明永乐年间（1403～1424年）制作。佛位于莲花中心，莲瓣可以开合，莲座纹饰精细绝伦。

Gilded 'Flower Presented to Buddha'　The carving, made during the reign of Yong Le (1403-1424), is kept in the Trilokya Hall. The Buddha sits in the center of a lotus blossom and the petals can be opened and closed.

宫藏经书　布达拉宫所藏经书甚丰，图为其一部分。

Buddhist scriptures　The Potala Palace keeps a great amount of Buddhist scriptures. The picture shows a part of them.

木雕十一面观音

Wooden statue of the Eleven-Faced Bodhisttva.

胜乐金刚双身像 胜乐金刚为藏传佛教五部金刚大法本尊之一，其像为四面，每面三目，十二臂，主臂抱明妃金刚亥母。

Twin-Bodied Vajra of Victory and Joy The divine guardian has four faces, each with three eyes. The two master arms of his 12 arms hold Haimu, wife of the Vajra.

加央佛　明代制作，通体鎏金，工艺精湛，造型生动。

Jamyang Buddha　The gilded statue was made during the Ming Dynasty (1368-1644).

玉雕八思巴 八思巴（1235～1280 年），藏传佛教萨迦派（花教）首领。1260 年元世祖忽必烈（1260～1294年在位）封其为国师，后又令其管理全国佛教事宜和藏族地区行政事务，成为西藏政教领袖。

Jade statue of Bagsba Bagsba（1235-1280）was chief of the Sa-kya-pa（Variegated）Sect. He was appointed Chief Councilor by Kublai（Emperor Tai Zu of the Yuan Dynasty, reigned from 1260 to 1294）in 1260 and put in charge of Buddhist affairs in the country and government affairs in Tibet.

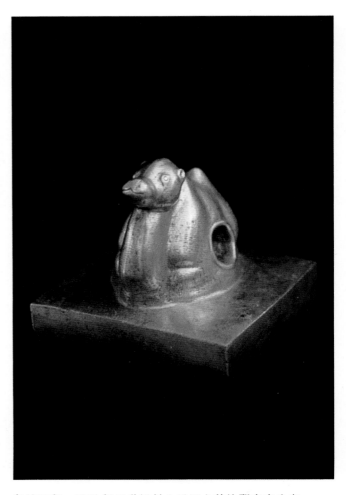

玉印 明朝（1368～1644 年）中央政府先后在西藏地区赐封大宝、大乘、大慈三大法王，图为 1413 年封萨迦派高僧昆泽思巴为大乘法王时所赐玉印。

Jade seal During the Ming Dynasty (1368-1644) the central government made three Dharma (Law) Kings in Tibet. The picture shows the jade seal of the Dacheng (Greater Vehicle) King of Law in 1413.

白兰王印 1264 年元世祖封八思巴之弟恰那多吉为白兰王，赐金印，并将公主墨卡顿许配给他。

Seal of King Bailan In 1264 Emperor Shi Zu (Kublai) of the Yuan Dynasty appointed Naduoji, younger brother of Bagsba, King of Bailan and married Princess Mokadun to him.

金印 为清顺治皇帝册封五世达赖喇嘛之印，印文用汉、满、蒙、藏四种文字刻铸。

Gold seal This is a seal conferred by Emperor Shun Zhi on the fifth Dalai Lama. The inscription is carved in the Chinese, Manchurian, Tibetan and Mongolian script.

金瓶　1793 年清乾隆皇帝 对 达 赖、 班 禅 转 世 实行 "金瓶掣签"措施，命制金瓶两尊供确认转世灵童掣签用，从此形成了百年不变的定制。金瓶一尊存北京雍和宫；另一尊原存拉萨大昭寺，后移至布达拉宫。瓶高 34 厘米，系纯金制作。

Gold bottle　In 1793 Emperor Qian Long of the Qing Dynasty made two gold bottles in which lots were drawn to decide who would be the successor of the Dalai Lama. The tradition lasted for the next 100 years. One of the gold bottle is kept in Yonghegong Lamasery in Beijing and the other is kept in the Potala Palace. The bottles of pure gold are 34 centimeters high.

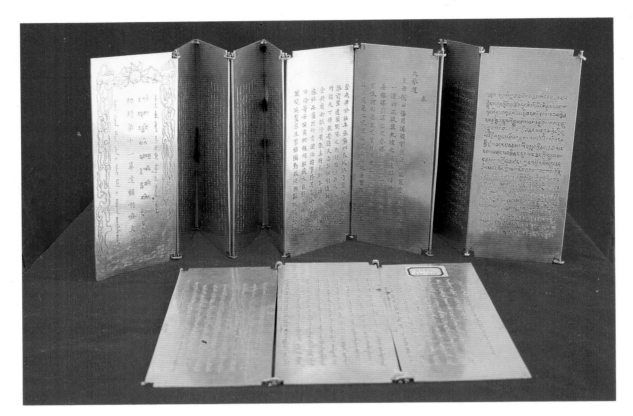

金册 1839 年，清道光皇帝（1820～1850 年在位）册封十一世达赖喇嘛的金册，用汉、满、蒙、藏四种文字书写。

Gold album In 1839 Emperor Dao Guang（reigned between 1820 and 1850）sent this mandate to confirm the 11th Dalai Lama. The text is written in the Chinese, Machurian, Tibetan and Mongolian script.

达赖喇嘛披风

Cloak of the Dalai Lama.

维修现场　Potala Palace under renovation.

维修与保护

　　布达拉宫自 17 世纪大规模扩修后，三百多年间未进行全面整修。因此，尽管其外观雄伟依旧，殿堂内部却多处废圮。中国政府十分重视布达拉宫的维修和保护，1959 年以后即常年拨付维修经费。1988 年决定拨巨资全面整修。次年 10 月隆重开工，历时近五年，至 1994 年 8 月竣工，西藏僧俗为此在拉萨市举行了盛大的庆典活动。

Maintenance and Protection

　　The Potala Palace had not undertaken any overall repairs since its reconstruction in the 17th century. Though it retained it outer grandeur the interior had fallen in disrepair. In 1959 the central government established a special fund for regular maintenance of the Potala Palace and in 1988 decided to give it an overhauling. The gigantic project began in October the following year and finished in August 1994. A grand unveiling ceremony was held amidst jubilant.

维修前景象 布达拉宫维修前，一些殿堂地面下陷，梁柱倾斜，壁画龟裂。

The Potala Palace before the overhauling The foundation of the palace had subsided in parts; pillars went tilted and cracks appeared in wall paintings.

打夯的藏族工匠 布达拉宫的地面和殿堂的平顶用藏地特有的阿嘎土铺设，这种土经反复夯打，坚固而光亮。

Rammers on the worksite The floors and flat roofs of the Potala Palace are paved with a local clay, very solid after repeated ramming.

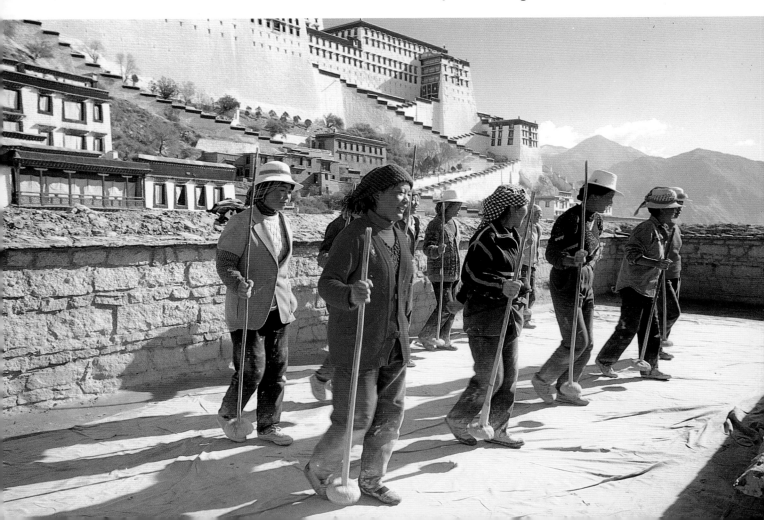

诵经祈祷 维修工程得到藏族僧俗的支持。在维修期间，宫内僧人每月按宗教仪规举行祈祷仪式，祝愿工程顺利进行。

Lamas chanting prayers The overall repair of the Potala Palace was supported by the clergy and laymen alike. The lamas of the palace held regular services to pray for its success.

修饰一新的大殿内顶 维修中严格遵循国家文物保护法，保持建筑原貌。

Ceiling of a grand hall after repair The central government set strict regulations for the repair so that the Potala Palace would retain its original appearance.

修缮后的檐下斗拱

Brackets under the eave after repair.

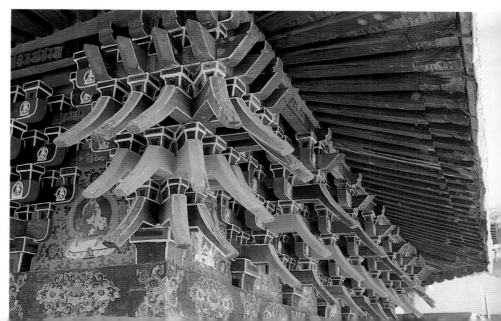

◀ **庆典盛况**　为庆贺布达拉宫维修竣工，拉萨市僧俗在德阳厦举行盛大庆典，图为跳驱魔神舞的情景。

Celebrating the completion of the repair　Lamas and common people in Lhasa held a grand ceremony for the completion of the project. The picture shows a dance to ward off evils during the celebration.

表演牦牛舞

Yak Dance during the celebration.

庆祝维修竣工的佛事活动

Buddhist service in celebration of the repair project.

庆典盛况　为庆贺布达拉宫维修竣工，拉萨市僧俗在德阳厦举行盛大庆典，图为跳驱魔神舞的情景。

展佛 是一种仪式，寺庙将珍藏的大佛像挂出，供信徒祈祷和膜拜，意为佛来到人间普渡众生。为庆贺维修竣工，在布达拉宫前举行了盛况空前的展佛仪式。

Display of the Buddha To display portraits of the Buddha is a long tradition of the Potala Palace. To celebrate the completion of the repair project, the treasured portraits were put out for the people to admire.

狂欢之夜 欢乐的人群在布达拉宫前跳起了藏族古典舞蹈，狂欢活动持续到深夜。▶

Jubilant night Merry-making crowds in Lhasa dance ancient Tibetan dances throughout the night to celebrate the completion of the repair project of the Potala Palace.

面佛顶礼 展佛时垂挂的两幅巨大锦绣佛像是布达拉宫重宝，平时收藏宫中，举行展佛仪式时人们争相瞻仰，顶礼膜拜。

Buddha portraits The two huge portraits of the Buddha are embroidered on brocade. They are displayed only on grand occasions.

（京）新登字号 131 号

编　　辑　南　卉
翻　　译　刘宗仁
责任编辑　望天星　施永南
摄　　影　土　登　觉　果　戚　恒　马竞秋
　　　　　杜泽泉　陈宗烈　康　松
装帧设计　蔡　荣

Editor: Nan Hui
Translated by Liu Zongren
Editors-in-charge: Wang Tianxing and Shi Yongnan
Photos by Tudeng, Jueguo, Du Zequan, Chen Zonglie,
Qi Heng, Kang Song and Ma Jingqiu
Designed by Cai Rong

图书在版编目（CIP）数据

布达拉宫：中英文/南卉编；刘宗仁译. —北京：中国
世界语出版社，1995．8
　　ISBN 7－5052－0243－X

　　I. 布… 　II. ①南… ②刘… 　III. 布达拉宫－画册－
汉、英　IV. B947－64

中国版本图书馆 CIP 数据核字(95)第 12106 号

布达拉宫
南　卉　编
*
中国世界语出版社出版
北京 1201 厂印制
中国国际图书贸易总公司(国际书店)发行
1995 年 8 月(16 开)第一版第一次印刷
ISBN 7－5052－0243－X／K・39 (外)
13800
85－CE－464S